I0486775

Increase Your Career Possibilities

An Insider's Guide to Interview Success

Sari Neudorf

SDN Consulting

authorHOUSE®

AuthorHouse™
1663 Liberty Drive, Suite 200
Bloomington, IN 47403
www.authorhouse.com
Phone: 1-800-839-8640

© 2009 SDN Consulting. All rights reserved.

No part of this book may be reproduced, stored in a retrieval system, or transmitted by any means without the written permission of the author.

First published by AuthorHouse   3/27/2009

ISBN: 978-1-4389-6272-6 (e)
ISBN: 978-1-4389-6273-3 (sc)

Library of Congress Control Number: 2009902246

Printed in the United States of America
Bloomington, Indiana

This book is printed on acid-free paper.

Increase Your Career Possibilities

Introduction

If you're like me, you're probably wondering how the majority of people you work with find their way to the office every day. But somehow they continue to get hired, while you do the yeoman's share of the work.

Here is the reason why: *they know how to interview.* It is as simple as that.

The goal of this book is to bridge the gap between success in interviewing and success in the workplace, with the ultimate goal of getting hired.

Think back to the hard work you initially put into your current job. Your success there didn't happen overnight. You probably failed once or twice before you got it. The same holds true with interviewing. However, as you have probably discovered, there aren't as many opportunities in today's employment market to hone your interview skills. Yet, it's important to be spectacular from the beginning. Have you ever heard of getting a mulligan on an interview? I didn't think so.

Consider the amount of time you spent researching any big purchase you've made—how many people you checked with to see what's the best on the market; how many buyers' guides you read; how many items you test drove, sampled, tried on, or borrowed before you made the final decision. It only makes sense to do this much prep work before interviewing, too. Not every opportunity is the right one for you—and there's no return policy when you take the wrong job. The sale is final and will probably be included on your new résumé. And, if it isn't, you will need to explain the time gap between one job and the next. So, being prepared to make the best decision is very important.

I have successfully coached, guided, and written résumés for clients based on twenty years' worth of real-life experience. From fitness instructors, psychologists, housewives, and nontraditional salespeople to career changers, downsized employees, and college graduates: all have benefited from my assistance. Most have gone on to attain their career desires. They all will agree that knowing what to expect and how to respond was empowering—and that preparing before every interview made the difference between just getting a job and choosing a great career.

This book will take you from writing your résumé to accepting the job. Now, let's take a look at what it's going to take for you to get that job offer.

Appearance

Guess what? What you've heard about only getting one opportunity to make that first impression is true. So make certain that you look great. That means looking like that company's brand. You really don't want the hiring manager to wonder whether or not you own a mirror, or if you are splitting your time among cocktail waitress, sports coach, and potential interviewee.

When you're targeting a company, you might consider visiting the workplace or meeting with others who work there to check out the company's brand image. Once you look like the brand, you'll be ahead of the competition. People like to hire those who look like they do. Be a mirror so that they see you as their new candidate. Dress for the position that you want to have. Get a power suit that makes you feel successful and, yes, powerful. If you feel it, your energy will be positive, and you'll come across as the best candidate for the position. Have that special suit ready to go, and only use it for interviews. You may wear the same suit to all interviews as long as it's in great condition, clean, pressed, and represents the successful person you are.

For both men and women, a dark-colored suit (black or navy, without pinstripes) paired with a simple white shirt is a good choice. Men should make certain that their shoes are dark-colored and polished. Wingtip shoes or conservative loafers are never out of style. Tie color also should be simple. You want the interviewer to concentrate on your answers and successes you bring to the company, not your choice of attire.

It's also essential to be well-groomed. Get a manicure and a haircut. If you have a beard or a mustache, make sure it is neat and trimmed. Your goal is to create a first impression of an individual who cares about the entire package.

For women, "simple" also is the key. Simple jewelry, classic shoes (pumps are a great choice), and neutral-colored stockings work in your favor. Whether to choose pants or a skirt is always a dilemma. The choice is yours; in either case, the goal is to wear a *power suit*. You are applying for a position of integrity. Don't confuse looks with credentials. It's a job interview, not a date. Do you want to look like a working girl, or a girl who works? If you're hired, you're a walking advertisement for the company—and they want someone who is an extension of their mission statement. Less is always best.

It's also important to consider what *not* to bring to the interview. If the person sitting across from you wonders what your thought process was prior to leaving the house, well, you have lost the opportunity to be hired. This means that any adornment other than an American flag pin is in bad taste. The silicone bracelet and extra earrings or rings need to be removed before the interview. Your goal is to be a blank canvas, devoid of any personal or political advertising

Remember, every company has a formula by which they hire; once you master it, you are that much closer to your new job. Try this: walk through a shopping mall and notice the employees who are on break. If they were all placed in a line-up, you could pick out the store each person was associated with by his or her attire. That's the point: be the *brand*. Every company has a brand. Think about logos, symbols, and company names that spark immediate recognition. At every company with which you interview, be *their* brand in your appearance, and you'll have one less hurdle to overcome on your way to a job offer.

Résumés and Templates

The purpose of a résumé is to highlight your skills, qualifications, and successes that are in sync with the position you seek. It is the bait you use to capture your audience—a.k.a. your future boss. Don't confuse your résumé with your autobiography. The goal is to have the reader see your successes and conclude that you deserve an opportunity for a face-to-face interview.

There are many different styles, strategies, and opinions that can be implemented in the construction of a résumé. Remember, most managers are going to be reviewing your résumé late at night. This means you need to remember to "KISS": keep it simple, stupid. Allow the reader to see your achievements at first glance. If the manager or interviewer has to pull it out of you, it's probably more work than they want to put into you.

Your résumé is an outline of your career accomplishments. It does not replace a face-to-face interview. Every line should answer the question, "So what?" If you need to be present to explain anything on your résumé, your résumé probably isn't well-written. The competition is fierce. Résumés that receive the coveted call to interview highlight successes and transferable skills that will be beneficial to your future manager. Make your résumé work for you.

The font and paper that you choose for your résumé are as important as the suit you wear to the interview. The majority of companies are conservative. They hire people who reflect their *brand*. It is simple to become the peg for their hole. Begin with a recognizable, universally compatible font; Times New Roman, Arial, Tahoma, and Book Antiqua are preferred. Font size should never be smaller than twelve points. Paper needs to be white, light ivory, or soft beige; the best choice is standard twenty-four-pound résumé paper. If the paper has a watermark, the imprint should face the reader. Be proud of your accomplishments. Hand prospective employers a paper that reflects that pride.

The same standards hold true for electronic versions of your résumé. You can either send your résumé as a file attachment in Microsoft Word, ASCII text, PDF, or as a Web layout. The goal is for your recipient to open a file that is clear, clean, and readable.

Organizing Your Employment History

Résumés can be written in three different formats: chronological, functional, or career profile, which is a combination of the first two.

The chronological résumé is a timeline of employment, with dates and responsibilities presented in descending order. This is the preferred format when there are no time gaps in employment history.

The functional résumé is best suited for those who have had several jobs—more than three within five years—or gaps in employment history.

The career profile is used for the "seasoned" job hunter, someone who possesses numerous transferable skills and who has achieved clear, documented results in multiple industries.

No matter which style you choose, the number one rule is to hit them with your best shot up front. The job advertised might be for a hunter; that doesn't mean the hiring manager wants to hunt for your "money skills" on your résumé. Begin with your most current position, highlighting all your accomplishments and responsibilities. Focus on the elements that make you marketable for the job you want to have. These might include increased sales; work as a field trainer, project leader, division co-chairman, or editor of the district newsletter; and any awards you received that set you apart from others in your field.

You also should highlight skills that you have either acquired on your own or as part of training within an organization. Computer skills are always good to include; this is code for your ability to work effectively and efficiently. Have you taken any management training, public speaking, or selling-skills courses? Include any special training you've had that would help boost you above the competition.

End your résumé with your education, degrees held, and, in some instances, your GPA. Remember that some companies will verify your degree and the institution you attended. Some companies do not conduct background checks until after you have been hired. I have seen many people fired *after* three or four months on the job for falsifying this information.

If you don't have a degree but the job requires one, well, my friend that is just not going to work for you. Better that you learn this early in the game. There are plenty of other opportunities out there for you. Choosing the job that is the right fit is *your* job.

Here's the rule of thumb for GPAs: if it's not above a 3.0, consider leaving it off. Some companies really care about this number; these are the companies that have a hiring formula. The good news is that if you fit the formula, then this is probably a good job for you. The bad news is that if you don't, it's like buying a pair of shoes a half size too small—it will be painful and never a good fit.

End your résumé with this phrase: "References available upon request." Do not include references with your résumé. Let the HR representative ask for your references. That means he or she is interested in moving you forward in the process. You also might think about customizing your references to the job. If you're applying for a medical sales position that involves selling orthopedic products, you might want to use your friend the doctor as a reference. Having people with the strongest name recognition is a good move.

As with everything else, call and prepare your references before they are contacted. I hate surprises, and so should you. Make certain your references will talk you up and give you a glowing report. I coach job seekers to have a friend contact their references pretending to be an HR manager to find out exactly what type of information the references are giving their future employers. Not everyone is on the same page with you or has your best interests in mind when the phone rings, so be proactive.

> TIP: Well-written résumés get an immediate response—usually a phone call within two weeks. If weeks pass without any contact, your résumé needs to be revisited and reworked—or you might be applying for jobs that are out of your league.

Résumé Templates
Chronological résumé template

CAROL JONES
456 State Street, Chicago, IL 66343
cjones@hotmail.com
618/888–9898

CAREER OBJECTIVE or SUMMARY
Describe the position you are seeking and what qualifications you bring to the company.

EMPLOYMENT HISTORY
Company Name, City, and State
Your job title   **Dates of employment**
Responsibilities include: (describe what you do, for whom you do it, and where you do it).
- If you work with big, recognizable company names, include them here.
- Include your ranking among others in your company.
- List any awards received.
- Include anything else that is quantitative and showcases you as a top performer.

EDUCATION
University of Missouri, Columbia, Missouri
Bachelor of Science, Business Administration, 2002
Cum laude graduate

SKILLS, AWARDS, CERTIFICATES, LICENSES, AFFILIATIONS
- Computer skills
- Toastmasters International
- Real Estate license
- Eagle Scout

References available upon request.

Functional résumé template

CAROL JONES
456 State Street, Chicago, IL 66343
cjones@hotmail.com
618/888–9898

SUMMARY
Successful manager with superior skills and experience in delivering documented results in the manufacturing industry.

ACCOMPLISHMENTS IN LEADERSHIP
- Hired, trained, and coached two teams to deliver product in timely manner.

ACCOMPLISHMENTS IN OPERATIONS MANAGEMENT
- Delivered completed project 15 percent under budget.

EMPLOYMENT HISTORY
Company name, city, and state
Your position and/or title   **Dates of employment**

EDUCATION
University of Missouri, Columbia, Missouri
Bachelor of Science, Business Administration, 2002

SKILLS, AWARDS, CERTIFICATES, LICENSES, AFFILIATIONS
- Computer skills
- Toastmasters International
- Real Estate License
- Big Brothers Big Sisters

References available upon request.

Pre-Interview Checklist

Being 100 percent prepared for every opportunity builds confidence that lets your potential boss know that you are the person to hire. Preparation means that you listen, read, and do your research before you accept any phone screens or face-to-face interviews.

Below is a checklist to prepare you for the interview. Every answer can be obtained from either the job description or the recruiter who contacts you.

- **Company name**

- **Name of interviewer**

- **Product names**

- **Territory/location**

- **Job requirements:** type of sales, prior years of experience, type of industry

- **Job qualifications/transferable skills:** organizational, rapport building, documented sales results, in-servicing, presentations, team building

- **Preparing for the questions**
  - Strength (core competency)
    Situational story
  - Strength (core competency)
    Situational story
  - Strength (core competency)
    Situational story

- **Questions to ask during the interview**

- **Closing for the next step:** have two goals prepared for the close.

Interview Protocol and Structure

Interviews, and the overall process used to determine if you are the "right hire," are conducted using either behavioral- or situational-style questions. The setting can be a formal office or conference room, a hotel, or a restaurant.

> TIP: It's an interview. Don't lose focus because you're eating lunch and joking around with your future boss.

You are in your power suit, it's an interview, and your goal is to get the job. Their goal is to hire the candidate who can do the best job and bring results. They are not interviewing for a new best friend. Don't be confused by their friendly demeanor. Remember, you are there to convince them that you have every skill they are looking for in their new hire.

Behavioral-style questions begin with, "Tell about me a time when ..." Sometimes the interviewer produces a yellow legal pad; as you answer, the interviewer checks the competencies (we'll cover those later) that you've articulated. Hiring managers need to have objective reasons why they want to hire you. Once you've said the magic words (mentioned the right core competencies), you move to the head of the class.

Situational style is geared towards hypothetical situations and problem solving. You may be asked about a situation that you've never encountered, and you may feel unable to respond because of your lack of experience. But it's not that you lack experience with the situation—you lack the ability to *decode the question* and come up with the correct competency.

Here's an example: let's say you're questioned about a leadership project, and you hear the question as, "What leadership experiences have you had?" But the question is really about focus, and whether or not you are capable of conducting checks to keep you on track toward a goal. Guess what? You probably have dozens of stories with great outcomes that you can discuss. Knowing how to decode interview questions and understand what is being asked will move you forward with confidence.

The Interview Process

It goes like this:

Someone from the company contacts you by phone or e-mail to either:

1. Set up a time for a face-to-face interview, or
2. Arrange a time for a phone screening.

Phone screening is common in many industries. The upside of a phone screen is that your résumé is working for you. Companies that are hiring a large number of people at one time want to find qualified candidates by weeding out those who are not so qualified. A phone screen usually includes a review of your résumé, some basic questions about why you're interviewing, a request for any questions you might have, and, hopefully, the guarantee of a face-to-face interview in the near future.

TIP: Keep a log of all job opportunities for which you've sent in your résumé. For each company, include the correct pronunciation of the company's name, the products they sell, contact names, and the salary they offer. When opportunity calls, this preparation will pay off big time.

A great phone screener will validate your salary requirement before scheduling a face-to-face interview. It just doesn't make sense for a company to have you come in when the salary they offer is below your financial requirements. This is the only time money should be discussed prior to a job offer. You need to make certain that both the job and the money are a good fit for you. A great job without the proper pay is called "volunteer work."

OK, the day of the big interview is here. You are totally empowered in your power suit. You have five clean copies of your résumé on sturdy résumé paper; you have your portfolio of accomplishments bound and ready; and you've arrived fifteen minutes early. Throw out your gum and pop in a breath mint.

Take a deep breath and get ready to shine.

1. Enter the room and ask politely where you can sit. Interviewing is like a dance, and there are certain steps for success. Proper interview etiquette means always asking before doing. This shows that you have manners and will not embarrass the company if you are hired.
2. Most interviews begin with an overview of your résumé. Always begin at the bottom of the résumé with your education, and work your way up to present-day employment.
3. If a "sales pitch" is needed to get you on board with the company, the interviewer will use this opportunity to sell the benefits of working for this company.
4. Next comes everyone's favorite section: the questions designed to uncover your unique skills and core competencies.
5. After this, you'll be asked if you have any questions for the interviewer.
6. Now present your portfolio, brag book, or successes from previous positions.
7. Share your strategic business plan.
8. Close the interview by asking for the job.
9. Thank the person with a handwritten note.

This is the basic interview formula. The length of time varies from thirty minutes to one hour, depending on how many interviews are conducted prior to hire. Each company has its own brand and style.

Some organizations require you to take personality tests before a phone screen. I've even heard of companies scheduling five different interviews prior to hire. The good news is that you'll be prepared, regardless of the length of time or number of interviews required.

The Questions

Before we look at *what* types of questions can be asked during an interview, let us look at the *why*. What are the questions trying to uncover? What is the purpose of sitting across from a stranger who is not your therapist and discussing how your mind works? And where do they come up with these questions?

Here's the simple answer. Companies use either their HR departments or other sources to develop questions that, when answered in certain ways, will demonstrate that you understand the core competencies necessary to be successful in the company. Your goal during the interview is to convince your potential boss that you will perform better than anyone they have ever hired. To do this, you need to know the "secret words" that the interviewer is waiting to hear you insert into every answer. Those secret words are the *transferable skills* and *core competencies* that will move you to the head of the class.

The world has become very politically correct. Giving a candidate the time-honored thumbs up is not a good enough reason to hire someone. Companies today depend on objective scoring of each candidate's responses to validate hiring decisions.

Knowing what *you* consider to be the right answer to every question just won't cut it. Knowing why *they* are asking—and what the secret words are—will.

It is an understatement to say that today's employment arena is highly competitive. But if you know in advance the transferable skills and core competencies that the company deems essential, that knowledge will clarify questions and assist you in formulating responses and maintaining control of the interview.

> TIP: Just as your current employer has trained you to present their product in the best light, so should you present yourself when answering interview questions. Promoting the desirable skills to get the job is called survival.

Many companies have looked at their best employees, the cream of the crop, and come to the conclusion that the best of the best all have similar skills and competencies prior to being hired. They come to the table with a positive attitude, superior communication skills, a strong work ethic, the drive to learn the product better than anyone else, and the persistence to get the job done. The sooner you understand these core competencies and how to verbally demonstrate them during the interview process, the sooner you will be on your way to your new position.

> TIP: One commonality among all new hires is their lack of knowledge in the marketing strategies and product knowledge of the company.

> TIP: The other commonality among all new hires is their knowledge of sales and their attainment of goals.

Below are categories of core competencies and a description of what each looks like in the workplace. It's a good idea to compose your situational stories to fit these areas.

> TIP: —Your ultimate goal is to include every core competency in your answers so that you can move forward in the interview process.

Customer Orientation

- You are able to read the customer.
- Your selling strategies are specific to each customer and delivered at the customer's pace.
- You don't walk in with your agenda hanging out.
- Customers look forward to seeing you and make time to talk because of the sense of purpose you bring to them.
- You are the only rep the customer sees.
- You are the envy of your company because you turn the no into a yes.

Focus

- You are the person with a plan at every turn.
- You set measurable, attainable goals that keep you intensely self-motivated.
- Your eye is always looking past the goal line.
- Along with a daily to-do list, you have weekly, monthly, and yearly priority goals set to propel you forward.
- Your world includes spreadsheets, sales rankings, contest awards, and letters from bosses commending you on consistently exceeding goals.
- You work smart and meet all deadlines.
- When asked to describe your greatest achievement, your answer covers the clear and deliberate steps taken to deliver.

Ego

- You are driven by your own definition of what "success" looks like.
- You consistently rank in the top 10 percent or higher within your company. You rise to the height of your own bar.
- You are independent and confident of your ability and skills to be the best.
- You strive for recognition as a leader, "top dog," and the "go-to" person in all situations.
- You are the person singled out at every national sales meeting as the one to catch.
- It's not the money that drives you.

- This is how you are wired.
- You are an altruistic individual, working for the cause.

Ability to be an Activator
- You make it happen.
- You are clear, direct, and aggressive in your ability to get others on board with your way of thinking.
- You are persistent and not easily put off.
- You capitalize on past relationships, taking trust to a new level and completing the sale.

Individualized Perception
- You "listen" to your customers, uncovering their uniqueness.
- Your selling strategy is specific to each customer's benefit.
- You are innovative and creative in your selling approach.
- Consultative in nature, you are skilled at moving the customer through the selling model and closing the sale.

Ability to be an Arranger
- You are a born leader.
- You look at all sides of the situation to uncover the best way to get things done.
- You think through situations to generate appropriate solutions rather than overreact.
- Your toolbox is filled with feedback from your boss and "best practices" from others.

Ability to be a Stimulator
- You were voted "Most Convivial" in school.
- Mention your name, and people think, "Enthusiastic, optimistic, and passionate."
- If you walked into Cheers, everyone would shout your name.
- You frequently distribute praise, recognizing the success of others around you.

- As a natural cheerleader, you find that one product that is in need of resuscitation, and generate superior sales by building a buzz.

Interpersonal Relationships
- You understand that people buy from those whom they like; you are a firm believer in building rapport.
- You have never met a stranger.
- Your mental database contains the "unnoticed" changes in the office staff: haircuts, vacations, birthdays.
- You have woven yourself into the office fabric.

Discipline
- You are structured in your approach to work.
- You have superior organizational and time-management skills.
- Clients know that you will return their phone call within one hour because of your follow-up skills.
- You are dependable and, as my father-in-law says, "If you can't be on time, be early" is your motto in everything you do.

Trust
- This is the end result of all of the above competencies.
- You work at building credibility, being honest with customers.
- You consistently follow through on all commitments and correspondence.
- Your work ethic is a reflection of who you are. It is your *brand*.

If selling is your passion (and really, isn't everyone in some sort of sales?), you have already recognized these traits or competencies in yourself. They are the basic skills, the Sales 101 syllabus, that make the best the best. If this doesn't sound like you, perhaps this is not the career move for you.

The 60-Second Connection

Great: you've made it to your first face-to-face interview! This means your résumé has passed the first in a long line of tests or interviews. You now have the opportunity to show off all your transferable skills and core competencies during an interview. Your résumé is written to highlight the successes your new employer wants to see. In the same vein, your verbal communication style should be tailored to the person who will be interviewing you.

What does this mean to you? There is an incredible phenomenon that happens when you connect with people. You know what I mean. You walk into a sales meeting and begin working the room. You probably migrate to the individual who is dressed like you, or perhaps they remind you of a good friend. The conversation begins, and within five minutes, you're laughing and talking as if you've known each other for years. You have so many things in common, you wonder if you were separated at birth! You speak the same language with ease and confidence.

What you have done without realizing it is make a "me too" connection. It is the like-attracts-like phenomenon. Out of all the people in that room, you were drawn to your "mirror."

I bet you're asking yourself what you should do when the person who is interviewing you is not a reflective mirror, but rather a "funhouse" mirror? Don't panic. Below are descriptions of the four types of people you might encounter during your interview. The best way to make that me-too connection is to learn the language of the people who will interview you. Just as you tailor your sales calls—working at the pace of each customer, identifying where each is in the sales model—so, too, do you need to do this with the person across the table from you. But, it takes time to build this database of information, and you don't have time to cultivate, cajole, and develop your skills in the thirty minutes granted at your first interview.

Below is a "code sheet" that identifies basic characteristics of each type of person who is likely to be sitting across from you during an interview. After you read each description, take a moment to revisit some of the people in your life who fit into each category. Put a face and name with each personality type.

Direct

Looks like: Business— meaning they are dressed in conservative colors and styles (nothing flashy, just basic Brooks Brothers), and well groomed. Direct people take pride in their appearance because of their competitive natures, and because their appearance affects the way people view them in the workplace. They have high egos and like to be reminded that they are smart.

Behavior in the workplace: Direct people are able to make decisions quickly. They know up front whether or not they are going to hire you. Directs will fight for their causes or ideas to be understood. They are to-the-point, results-oriented people. Their organizational skills are efficient, but not neat and orderly. They are considered high risk takers; they will hire the out-of-the-box candidate if he or she speaks their direct, results- based language.

During the interview: Be brief and to the point. Don't ramble or repeat yourself. Focus on the questions asked, and give succinct responses. Answers need to have quantitative and qualitative information. Do not make broad generalizations. Clearly articulate your strongly transferable skills. Highlight your ability to problem solve, achieve results, multitask, and get the job done quickly. Write down your goals, and bring the list with you to the interview. And, don't be concerned if a Direct interrupts your interview with phone calls, or changes the direction of the question while you're in mid- answer. Once Directs have the information they need to make a final decision, it's a done deal.

Influential

Looks like: Business with a flair for style—though not trendy. An Influential's business suit, albeit conservative, likely has a fancy handkerchief peeking out of the jacket pocket. And the cuff links in an Influential's French-cuff shirt are bolder than the average gold-colored initial disc. Influentials have a warm, friendly smile. They are welcoming, entertaining, social, talkative, emotional, and enthusiastic.

Don't be misled. They respect the bottom line and want every duck in a row.

Behavior in the workplace: Influentials are impulse decision-makers. Their desks are disorganized, with piles of unrelated information and unopened envelopes. They are warm and friendly people, focused and trusting—until crossed. Although they are not good at setting goals, they require this skill in others. They are moderate risk takers who make the rules up as they go along.

During the interview: Be friendly and agreeable. Let an Influential know that you can be coached (because Influentials can't be). Be articulate, focused, and to the point in all your answers. Stay on task. Give clear responses to questions, and don't offer any filler. Give too much information, and you'll lose an Influential. Be sure to talk about being a team player.

Steady

Looks like: Probably the same as ten years ago. Clothing is in good condition, but not *GQ* or *Vogue* inspired. Steadys' physical appearance is as durable, practical, and efficient as Steadys are in the workplace. They are good listeners, patient, and loyal. They are into closure.

Behavior in the workplace: Steadys are masters of the poker face, difficult to read during interviews. They are not quick-decision-on-the-spot types, and they need time to mull over information before answering. "I'll get back to you" is a common phrase among Steadys. Don't push a Steady into an answer too early, or you will have lost the sale. Steadys do not embrace change easily; they are systematic in organizational skills, but default to time-tested skills and rules.

During the interview: Be personable and agreeable, but not aggressive. Discuss your ability to build rapport, and your incredible follow-up skills. Talk about how task-focused you are, and how you value proven procedures to attain success. Steadys respect dependability, patience with others, and strong team-player skills. Answers need to be clear, direct, and full circle. Talk about results.

Compliant

Looks like: A classic, dressed in a functional, well-made business suit. Compliants are rule followers who are concerned about the bottom line, details, and the logical steps to get results. Social skills and rapport building aren't as important as getting the job done. They may not have that look and air of success about them, but don't be fooled. They are highly intelligent.

Behavior in the workplace: Very slow to make decisions. Compliants are analytical rule followers who need clear, direct goals, and who like to hear that in their co-workers as well. They are very, very organized, and they don't like change. Compliants are driven to be prepared, educated, qualified, and informed. No piece of information is too inconsequential. They are not fans of chitchat.

During the interview: Be direct and to the point. You are an agreeable, not argumentative individual who believes in win-win, not conflict. Have all your success stories prepared in advance, and be clear. Discuss the path you took and how you set goals. Support your statements with accurate data. You need to be organized; logical, not emotional; and able to keep it one hundred percent business. If a Compliant's question appears to be confrontational, recognize that it is a fact-finding question, not an integrity question. It's not personal—it's business.

When you enter the room for your interview, you will clearly see one of these four personalities. The take-away is to realize that some people need quick, direct answers; they want the job done without questions, problems, or detours. Others want to know that once you're hired, you'll be dependable, task-focused, and a list maker.

The goal here is not to change you, but rather for you to use this knowledge to get the most out of an interview. It's your way of making that me-too connection, of being the brand—and getting the job.

Prior to an interview, you need to formulate your situational answers. Review past experiences and work on clearly verbalizing your transferable skills that will be required in the new position.

Becoming familiar with the STAR formula and understanding which core competencies to include in your answers before you put your hand on the interview door is priceless.

> TIP: What you consider to be the "right" answer and what is the "right" answer are rarely the same.

STAR

This stands for *Situation, Task, Action, and Result.*

In other words, present information as though you are writing a newspaper article.

Situation: What is the title of the article?

Task: What skills did you utilize from your bag that helped you complete the project and reach your goal?

Action: What happened? What did you do that made the outcome successful? This is the most important part of your story, when you get to talk about the transferable skills that your new employer is looking to uncover about their new hire.

Result: What was the end result: money, commitment, promotion, and/or recognition?

It is important to relate how you dealt with the situation and what you learned through the experience. This is sometimes more valuable than the outcome.

The most important part of STAR is to follow the sequence in an organized manner and *sell yourself*!

Also, remember to ask the interviewer if he or she would like you to elaborate. And show enthusiasm!

Below are some sample questions that you will want to review and be prepared to answer if you are asked. The time to prepare your answers is *before* the interview. Select examples from your vast work experience to use in answering the following questions so that you can present yourself at your best during the interview. (You don't want to begin a scenario and realize halfway through that you should have chosen a different story to tell.)

- Why did you choose to work for your current company?
- Tell me about a time when you had to overcome obstacles in your job.
- Tell me about a project you accomplished in your current position. How did you do it? (Use any success story.)
- Why are you looking to change positions? (You might be hitting your head on the financial ceiling.)

- What do you like the most about your current position?
- What do you like the least?
- Why are you interviewing with this company?
- Who else are you interviewing with? (You prefer that those names remain confidential while you're in the interview process).
- What are your strengths and weaknesses?
- How do you work in a group situation?
- Did you ever have to put in more work to get the job done? (This is code for, "Do you go the extra mile, and can you think outside the box?")
- How do you perform under stress? Can you give an example of a time when this happened?
- Have you ever had to convince a superior on a project about which you felt strongly? What steps did you take?
- Tell me about a time you had to take a risk. What did it entail?
- Have you ever had difficulty working with a peer? How did you overcome that?
- Have you ever gone over your boss's head to get something accomplished?
- Are you working today?
- Have you ever been asked to do something unethical?
- How do you handle negative feedback?
- How has the industry changed?
- Have you ever had to change an initial goal to get better results?
- How do you prioritize your daily activities?
- How do you start your day? Give examples.
- Tell me about a time when you had to take no for an answer. How did you come to terms with the outcome?

- Where do you see yourself in the next five years? (This is code for, "If we hire you, will you stay with us longer than one year?")

Basically, any question that is asked is code for, "Tell me that you know how to follow protocol, that you can follow the chain of command, and that you understand the steps required to move successfully from point A to point Z."

You need to listen to all questions and answer clearly. You don't need to have canned answers. You do need to have your situational stories clear in your mind before the interview.

Remember, you are a successful person. Select your stories so you can go through the ABCs of a project and sell yourself. Make the interviewer want you to join the team and bring the same successes to his or her company.

Following are lists of additional questions. Sometimes the same questions are asked in different ways. Don't be confused. Review the questions and consider how they might come up in an interview. The basic core competency is listed either after each question or section to help you decode the question.

Remember, this is *your* interview, *your* story, and your opportunity to present yourself as the "right fit" for the company.

Behavioral-Style Interview Questions

- Give me an example of a time when you had to deal with a difficult customer. What happened? What did you do? *(Ability to be an Arranger)*
- When you have a multitude of things to do, how do you set your schedule? *(Discipline)*
- Tell me about a time when you had to make a quick decision that you were proud of? *(Ability to be an Arranger)*
- Tell me about something you have done that was creative. *(Individualized Perception)*
- Give me an example of an important goal you set, and explain how you achieved it. *(Focus)*

- Describe a time when you had to "roll with the punches." *(Individualized Perception)*
- Tell me about a job or task that was boring. How did you deal with it? *(Ability to be a Stimulator)*
- Give me an example of a time when you found a clever way of motivating a co-worker. *(Ability to be a Stimulator)*
- Tell me about a major obstacle that you encountered in your last job. How did you handle it? *(Discipline)*
- Give me an example of a miscommunication with a customer. How did you solve it? *(Focus)*
- Tell me about a time when a change of policy or a changed decision made your work difficult. What did you do? *(Focus)*
- Tell me about a time when you had to communicate unpleasant information to a co-worker or customer. What happened? *(Focus; Ability to be an Arranger)*
- Give me an example of a time when you had to make a decision without consulting your boss. What did you do? *(Focus; Discipline)*
- Tell me about a time when you had to make a decision even though you had too little information to easily arrive at a decision. What happened? *(Ego)*
- What types of things make you angry? How have you dealt with them? *(Customer Orientation)*
- You have explained that you are decisive and able to cope with most situations. Now tell me about a time when you had a problem you couldn't solve. *(Focus; Ability to be an Activator)*
- Tell me about a time when you had to change procedures to solve a problem. What did you do? *(Focus)*
- Tell me about a time when you made a decision although no policy existed to cover the situation. Explain. *(Focus)*

Organization and Planning Skills

- Describe a specific situation that illustrates how you set objectives to reach a goal.
- Tell me about a time when you had to choose between two or more important opportunities. How did you go about deciding which one was most important to you?
- Tell me how you normally schedule your time in order to accomplish your day-to-day tasks.
- Describe a situation where you had a major role in organizing an important event. How did you do it?
- Think about a lengthy term paper or report that you have written. Describe how you organized, researched, and wrote that report.
- Give an example of how you organized notes and other materials in order to study for an important exam.
- Describe a time when you reorganized something to be more efficient. How did you do it?
- Think of a time when you made important plans, only to have them derailed. How did you react? What did you do?

Interaction and Leadership

- Tell me about an event in your past that has greatly influenced the way you relate to people.
- Give a specific example that best illustrates your ability to deal with an uncooperative person.
- Some people have the ability to "roll with the punches." Describe a time when you demonstrated this skill.
- Tell me when you had to work with someone who had a negative opinion of you. How did you overcome this?
- Recall a time when you participated on a team. Tell me an important lesson you learned that is useful to you today.

- Describe an instance when you reversed a negative situation at school, work, or home. How did you do it?
- Describe a situation that best illustrates your leadership ability.
- Think about someone whose leadership you admire. What qualities impress you?

Assertiveness and Motivation

- Describe several work standards that you have set for yourself in past jobs. Why are these important to you?
- Tell me about a time when you experienced a lack of motivation. What caused this? What did you do about it?
- Describe a situation in which you had to deal with someone whom you felt was dishonest. How did you handle it?
- Describe a situation that made you extremely angry. How did you react?
- Tell me about a time that best illustrates your ability to "stick things out" in a tough situation.
- Describe a time when you motivated an unmotivated person to do something you wanted that person to do.
- Give me an example in which you were affected by organizational politics. How did you react?
- Give me an example in which someone tried to take advantage of you. How did you react?

Decision Making and Problem Solving

- Give me an example that illustrates your ability to make tough decisions.
- Tell me about a decision you made even though you did not have all the facts.
- Describe a situation in which you had to "stand up" for a decision you made that was unpopular.

- Describe a situation in which you changed your mind after you publicly committed to a decision.
- Describe a situation that illustrates your ability to analyze and solve a problem.
- Tell me about a time when you acted as a mediator to solve a problem between two other people.
- Describe a problem that seemed almost overwhelming to you. How did you handle it?
- Tell me about a time when you used a creative or unique approach to solve a tough problem.

The following general questions also will help recent grads prepare for employment interviews:

- Tell me a little about yourself.
- Why did you attend that particular college or university?
- What led you to choose your major or career field?
- What college subjects did you like best/least? What did you like/dislike about them?
- What has been your greatest challenge in college?
- Describe your most rewarding college experience.
- Do you think that your grades are a good indication of your academic abilities?
- If you could change a decision you made while at college, what would you change? Why?
- What campus involvements did you choose? What did you gain/contribute?
- What are your plans for continued or graduate study?
- What interests you about this job? What challenges are you looking for in a position?
- How have your educational and work experiences prepared you for this position?
- What work experiences have been most valuable to you? Why?

- Why are you interested in our organization? In what way do you think you can contribute to our company?
- How would you describe yourself?
- What do you consider to be your greatest strengths? Weaknesses? Give examples.
- If I asked the people who know you to give me one reason why I shouldn't hire you, what would they say?
- What accomplishments have given you the most satisfaction? Why?
- What are your long-range career objectives? How do you plan to achieve these?
- How would you describe your ideal job?
- What two or three things are most important to you in your job?
- Do you have a geographical preference? Why?

Traditional-Style Interview Questions

Warm-Up Questions (Focus)
- What made you apply for this position?
- How did you hear about this job opening?
- Briefly summarize your work history and education.

Work History (Individualized Perception)
- What special aspects of your work experience have prepared you for this job?
- Can you describe one or two of your most important accomplishments?
- How much supervision have you typically received in your previous job?
- Describe one or two of the biggest disappointments in your work history.
- Why are you leaving your present job? (Or, why did you leave your last job?)

- What is important to you in a company? What things do you look for in an organization?

Job Performance (Ability to be an Arranger; Discipline)
- Everyone has strengths and weaknesses as workers. What are your strong points for this job?
- In what areas would you say you need improvement?
- How did your supervisor on your most recent job evaluate your job performance? What were some of the good points and bad points of that evaluation?
- When you have been told there was a problem in your job performance, what have you typically done? Can you give me an example?
- Do you prefer working alone or in groups?
- What kind of people do you find it most difficult to work with? Why?
- Starting with your last job, tell me about any of your achievements that were recognized by your superiors.
- Can you offer an example of your ability to manage or supervise others?
- What are some things you would like to avoid in a job? Why?
- In your previous job, what kind of pressures did you encounter?
- What would you say is the most important thing you are looking for in a job?
- What are some of the things you feel you have done particularly well in your job, or in which you have achieved the greatest success? Why do you feel this way?
- What were some of the things about your last job that you found most difficult to do?
- What are some of the problems you encounter in doing your job? Which one frustrates you the most? What do you usually do about it?

- What are some things you particularly liked about your last job?
- Do you consider your progress on the job representative of your ability? Why?
- How do you feel about the way you and others in the department were managed by your supervisor?
- If I were to ask your present (or most recent) employer about your ability as a _____, what would he or she say?

Education (Ability to be an Arranger)

- What special aspects of your education or training have prepared you for this job?
- What courses in school have been of most help in doing your job?

Career Goals (Focus)

- What is your long-term employment or career objective?
- What kind of job do you see yourself holding five years from now?
- What do you feel you need to develop in terms of skill and knowledge in order to be ready for that opportunity?
- Why might you be successful in such a job?
- How does this job fit in with your overall career goals?
- Who or what in your life would you say influenced your career objectives most?
- Can you pinpoint any specific things in your past experience that affected your present career objectives?
- What would you most like to accomplish if you had this job?
- What might make you leave this job?

Creativity (Ability to be a Stimulator)
- In your work experience, what have you done that you consider truly creative?
- Can you think of a problem you have encountered for which the old solutions didn't work, and how you came up with new solutions?
- Of your creative accomplishments, big and small, what gave you the most satisfaction?
- What kind of problems have people recently called on you to solve? Tell me what you have devised.

Decisiveness (Focus; Individualized Perception)
- Do you consider yourself to be thoughtful and analytical, or do you usually make up your mind fast? Give an example.
- What was your most difficult decision in the last six months? What made it difficult?
- The last time you did not know what decision to make, what did you do?
- What was the last major problem with which you were confronted? What action did you take?

Range of Interests (Interpersonal Relationships)
- To what organizations do you belong?
- Tell me specifically what you do in the civic activities in which you participate. (Leading questions in selected areas, e.g., sports, economics, current events, finance.)
- How do you keep current with company changes?

Motivation (Ego)
- What is your professional goal?
- Can you offer examples of experiences on the job that you felt were satisfying?
- Do you have short- and long-term plans for your department? Are they realistic?
- Did you achieve those plans' goals last year?

- Describe how you determine the top priorities in the performance of your job.

Work Standards (Focus; Ego; Ability to be an Activator)
- What are your standards of success in your job?
- In your position, how would you define "doing a good job"? On what basis is your definition determined?
- When judging the performance of your subordinate, what factors or characteristics are most important to you?

Leadership (Ability to be a Stimulator)
- In your present job, what approach do you take to get your people together to establish a common approach to a problem?
- What approach do you take in getting your people to accept your ideas or departmental goals?
- What do you do specifically to set an example for your employees?
- How frequently do you meet with your immediate subordinates as a group?
- What sort of leader do your people feel you are? Do you agree with their opinion?
- How do you get people who do not want to work together to establish a common approach to a problem?
- Given the same scenario, if you do not have much time and the group's members hold seriously differing views, what would be your approach?
- How would you describe your basic leadership style? Give specific examples of how you practice this.
- Do you feel you work more effectively on a one-to-one basis or in a group situation?
- Have you ever led a task force, committee, or any group that didn't report to you, but from whom you had to get results? How did you do it? What were the

satisfactions and disappointments? How might you handle the job differently now?

Flexibility (Customer Orientation)

- What was the most important idea or suggestion you received recently from your employees? What happened as a result?
- What do you think about the continual changes in company operating policies and procedures?

Notes:

Questions to Ask the Interviewer

ny questions you ask during the interview need to be focused in two areas:

1. Questions that are specific to what you will be doing when you get hired. Have the interviewer begin thinking about *you* in the position. Ask about your first task as the company's new hire.

2. Questions that yield answers that can be used in the closing.

List your questions on a separate sheet of paper that you can bring out at the appropriate time. Some of the questions you might ask are:

- Why is this territory/position open?
- How did the territory do before the rep left?
- What do you think the most difficult component of the position will be?
- What do you see as the most challenging aspect of the position?
- What do you see as the first goal you want me to achieve in this position?
- What skills do you consider to be the most valuable for this position?
- How long has this territory been open?
- Who are the other people on the sales team in this district?
- How does my personality and skill set fit into the current district?

- What type of direct responsibilities will I have?
- What kind of product training can I expect?
- What is the skill set of your ideal rep?
- What is the hiring timeline?

Brag Book

Employers seek out the best of the best. Your goal is to highlight all your successes to help the interviewer know that you are an achiever and a sought-after future employee. Presenting a chronological history of documented successes is becoming an interview standard.

Before you close and ask for the job, you want to give the interviewer a stroll through your previous career successes and achievements. Below is a list of suggested items for you to compile and place in a presentation book. It's important to use the best possible materials to represent your achievements, because those materials reflect you. And you are one of the best.

Place these items in your brag book in descending chronological order, beginning with the most recent first.

- Current résumé
- Sales rankings
- Spreadsheets or graphs representing your sales achievements
- Signed copies of performance reviews
- Atta-Boy letters or emails
- Recommendations from past employers or customers
- Contest and award certificates
- Certificates of achievement or training certificates
- Copy of college diploma

There is no limit to the types of documentation you can use in the book. If you won a car for a year, but have no letter stating so, place a picture of yourself with the car in your book. I've seen people include pictures of themselves in Hawaii because they won a trip there as top reps in sales contests.

One of the goals of this presentation book is to brag about yourself by detailing all your wonderful achievements. This is not the time to be shy about your successes. You need to be clear that when this company hires you, you will deliver the same—and better—to your new employer.

The other goal is to show the interviewer that you are capable of presenting information in a clear and professional format to sell a product. In this case, the product is you.

Review all the information you have in your brag book with the interviewer. This is not the time to fumble or to seem confused. If asked a question about something in your book, *use a pen to point to the graphs and spreadsheets. This is what you will be asked to do once you are hired.* Make that first impression one of professionalism. Sell yourself like the product you will promote once hired. Let the interviewer know that *you* are the best person for the position; *you* are the one they want to hire.

Don't confuse your brag book with a photo album. Let the person flip through the book. If they have any questions, believe me, they will ask.

You can either leave your brag book, or not; it's your choice. Some companies do require a copy and should let you know that before your face-to-face interview.

Never put original certificates in your brag book. Keep a clean copy of the book for presentations; if you chose to leave books with interviewers, have photocopies made of the clean book and leave those .

> TIP: From this point, begin a file containing all recognition materials; awards; certificates; e-mails and letters; and descriptions of job responsibilities, dates included, to continually add to your brag book.

Closes

At the end of the interview, as with any transaction, it is most important that you ask for the job. This is accomplished with simple questions and confidence on your part.

You need to let the interviewer know that you are highly interested in working for the company. The following are basic questions and closes you can use.

At the end of the process, after you have reviewed your brag book and your strategic business plan, you will want to ask:

- Now that you have seen what I can offer [*name of company*], is there anything else you need to know about me before you offer me this position?
- Can I get a firm commitment from you today that you will be moving me forward in the interview process?
- I feel confident that [*name of company*] and I will be a good fit. What is your timeline for making your final decision and calling me with a job offer?
- Are there any unanswered questions or concerns you have about me that would prevent you from offering me the position today?
- What other information do you need to know about me before you can offer me this position?
- I'm very excited about this opportunity. What else do you need to know about me before you can offer me this position?
- I want you to know that this is position I want. Can I get a commitment from you that you will recommend me for this position and move me on to the next step?

- Can we agree that, if you are moving me forward in the interview process, I will hear back from you within forty-eight hours?

Obstacles and How to Overcome Them

One of the biggest mistakes you can make is to lose sight of the position for which you are applying. Remember that you are only competing with yourself. It doesn't matter whether you're the first or the last person to be interviewed: if your skills are right for the job, then you deserve to get the job. So *ask for it*!

Make certain that you have presented yourself in the best possible light and have had full opportunity to showcase all your successes from previous positions (use that brag book!). Your past success is what determines your marketability. Remember, your new employer wants to hire the best person for the job. You have spent the past hour or so reviewing the transferable skills that make you a successful candidate for the position. Certainly, your enthusiasm and desire to get hired should be apparent to whoever is interviewing you.

Another mistake is to lose control of the interview. If you allow the interviewer to focus on your past rather than on the current job skills required, you have lost control. You need to redirect the interviewer and bring the discussion around to what skills you can bring to the new position. Answer all questions by restating in various ways that the successes you have achieved in your current position are the same successes you will bring to this position. Help the interviewer to see you as the new hire. If the interviewer can see it, then you can be it. Be proactive and discuss the position in the present tense.

After you feel confident in closing, it is important that you thank the interviewer for his or her time and for the opportunity to interview for the position.

Depending on where the interview took place, you have two options:

- If the meeting occurred in a hotel venue, you can give the hotel receptionist your *handwritten* thank-you note and ask that it be delivered to the individual's room. Do not hand it to the person who interviewed you.

- If the meeting occurred in some other venue (a restaurant, office building, or conference room, for example—send the note through regular mail. Remember to bring a stamp with you so that you can address it properly—using the correct address from the interviewer's business card that you received at the beginning of the interview—and drop it in the mailbox on your way out.

You need to write a thank you note to everyone you came in contact with at the meeting. This means if three people interviewed you, then you need to write three thank-you notes.

The most important reason to send a thank you note—beyond expressing appreciation—is that it demonstrates your follow-up skills. *Do not omit this step in the interview process.* Your thank you note may not be the reason you get the job offer, but I can guarantee you won't be offered the job without one.

A thank you note can read like this:

Dear Sam,

Thank you for taking the time to interview me today. I look forward to my next step and to joining your team.

Sincerely,

Your name

I suggest that you write your note(s) before the interview so that you are certain to have them with you.

Strategic Business Plan

If done well, your performance during the interview process has demonstrated that you are a goal-focused individual. Both your past and future successes are based on your ability to be organized and have a game plan to reach the finish line. This is the purpose of the strategic business plan. Regardless of the company, product line, city, or end user to whom you will be selling, you can attain success because you know what success looks like.

The following pages have examples of strategic business plans that can be customized to address the daily performance specifics for any interview.

This is a powerful tool to bring to the interview. It sets you apart from the mediocre, clarifies your transferable skills that bring sales success, and answers the question, "Can you really do the job?"

My suggestion is to bring a strategic business plan to every interview. At every successive interview, add information that you learned from previous interviews to your plan. This shows your ability to learn and to go the extra mile even before you're hired.

TIP: Strategic Business Plans work. They are separate from your brag book and printed on résumé-type paper.

Below are some examples. *Do not copy them*. Use them to create plans that reflect your strengths.

Strategic Business Plan

First Thirty Days
- Review current call plan.
- Physically locate all offices and eliminate dead, retired, and/or relocated addresses.
- Learn office protocol.
- Develop itinerary based on office buying potential, and work on call frequency.

First Six Months
- Identify and target high-profile, high-purchasing customers.
- Get commitment to use these customers as referrals and references with future clients.
- Develop programs and/or meetings to increase dialogue with current and potential customers.

End of Year One
- Have commitment from high-potential clients to only purchase products manufactured by my company.
- Increase market share by 2 percent in metro area.
- Be considered a resource for product knowledge within current customer base.
- My territory ranked in top 5 percent of company.

Your Name
Strategic Medical Business Plan
Company Name
Date of interview

First Thirty Days

- Complete product training.
- Locate all offices within territory; introduce myself and discuss/review their needs as clients.
- Learn office protocol.
- Develop itinerary to maximize impact with reach and frequency.

First Six Months

- Contact referrals and gain access to demo product.
- Get commitment from current clients to expand territory referrals. Who do they know who would benefit from the product?

End of Year One

- Developed strong alliances with key end users in territory.
- Increase market share by 10 percent in area.
- Be considered a resource for [*therapeutic area*] within end-user setting.
- My territory ranked in top 5 percent of company.

Strategic (Hospital Based) Business Plan
Company Name
Date of Interview

First Thirty Days

- Learn product and marketing message.
- Review sales materials.
- Locate and make contact with existing customers.
- Develop itinerary and routing plan to see the most customers in the shortest time frame.

First Six Months

- Review office/hospital protocol.
- Identify core businesses and/or hospitals and physicians.
- Develop top twenty clients.
- Identify early adopters of product.
- Search out key decision leaders in territory and increase call frequency.

End of Year One

- Earn Rookie of the Year.
- Get commitment from end users to always purchase products from parent company.
- Find mentor in specific therapeutic arena.
- Increase territory sales by minimum of 5 percent across the board.

Strategic (Pharmaceutical Sales) Business Plan
Company Name
Date of Interview

First Thirty Days
- Set up individual files for all call-plan physicians and their staff.
- Create "Top Ten" and "Top Twenty" physician lists to develop as core business.
- Build an itinerary to encompass reach and call frequency for best ROI (return on investment).
- Organize sales aids, clinical studies, and premium items in car.
- Practice role playing to develop best presentation verbiage and increase comfort level.

First Six Months
- Have a strategic business plan for all call-plan physicians.
- Tweak routing to reflect any changes in office locations and hours.
- Develop list of physicians who have left area and names of physicians who replaced them.

End of Year One
- Select a physician mentor to increase disease-state knowledge.
- Join organizations affiliated with specific disease state.
- Gain a strong commitment from high-deciles physicians to prescribe product.

Strategic Business Plan (Pharmaceutical Sales)
Company Name
Date of Interview

First Thirty Days
- Develop initial routing by dividing call plan into zip-code order.
- Set goal of making fifteen calls per day among physicians and/or pharmacy groups.
- Use online resources, including the American Medical Association and WebMD, to verify phone numbers and directions.
- Call to confirm address and office hours.
- Complete product training.
- Practice presenting long and short sales calls using sales aids.
- Work on rapport-building skills with office staff.
- Organize home office and car.

First Six Months
- Develop "Top Ten" and "Top Twenty" lists of physicians.
- Complete strategic business plan for core business.
- Develop itinerary for best ROI; Top Ten reach and frequency weekly, at beginning of week.
- Continue to revise monthly itinerary to include all physicians on call plan.
- Become an expert in therapeutic area through continuing education.

End of Year One
- Earn "Rookie of the Year."
- Develop mentor relationship with thought leader in territory.
- Meet goal of 5 percent increase in sales across the board with physicians and/or hospitals.

Overview of Daily Activity as a Pharmaceutical Representative

- Communicate daily with voicemail and e-mails.
- Prioritize key physicians.
- Create territory business plan for attaining goals.
- Pre-call planning: set two goals for every call.
- Utilize marketing budget while adhering to PDMA guidelines.
- Review product information.
- Learn office protocol, including staff names and best times to call.
- Develop strategies to bring value to each call.
- Overcome the "no-see" doctor.
- Learn competition PI. (product insert)
- Gather prescription pricing and availability at local pharmacies.
- Role-play to address physician objections.
- Log call notes and transmit nightly to home office.
- Enter mileage and expenses daily into expense reports.
- Organize sales aids and scientific reprints in home office and car.
- Keep daily count of inventory.

Cover Letter Sample I

Dear [*name of contact person*] (or, "To whom it may concern"):

RE: (state the reference code and or the title position and city where you are applying.)

I am highly interested in the above sales position.

After reviewing my qualifications, I am confident that you will want to speak with me about this opportunity.

I consistently make a difference. I want to make a difference with your company.

I thank you in advance for taking the time to review my qualifications. I look forward to hearing from you in the very near future.

Sincerely,

Your Name

Cover Letter Sample II

Company Name
Address
Attention:

Dear [name of contact person],

I have been preparing myself for this opportunity for quite some time.

The required skills necessary to be successful in your organization represent the core competencies I have built into my skill base.

I am attaching my current résumé for you to review. I am confident that once you are familiar with my current and past successes, you will want to schedule a face-to-face interview with me.

My goal is to join an organization that will become my future home. Building brand integrity, representing a gold standard in the industry, and ultimately becoming the best salesperson within the company are the standards I strive to meet.

I thank you in advance for your time spent reviewing my résumé. I look forward to meeting with you and/or the hiring manager and joining your remarkable team.

Sincerely,

Your Name

About the Author

Sari Neudorf founded SDN Consulting in 2006. Before starting her own consulting firm, Neudorf partnered with national medical recruiting companies, writing résumés and instructing candidates on interview protocol and procedure. Her extensive knowledge comes from firsthand experience in the pharmaceutical and medical industries, where she held numerous positions. She began as a sales representative and worked her way up to a district manager position with multiple responsibilities.

Before embarking on her career in medical sales, she taught in the St. Louis County school system. She still holds a current teaching certificate in the state of Missouri.

Neudorf's credentials include a bachelor of arts in education from Stephens College, Columbia, Missouri. She is a certified professional résumé writer, certified employment interview consultant, and a certified professional behavioral analyst. She also is qualified to administer behavioral profile assessments to her clients.

Neudorf is a member of the board of the National Résumé Writers' Association. She also is a member of the Professional Association of Résumé Writers and Career Coaches, Career Development International, and ProfilingPro, Inc.

She continues her ongoing education in an ever-evolving industry. Her mission is to assist others in identifying their strengths and achieving their career goals.

Neudorf lives in St. Louis, Missouri, with her husband and two children.

Notes:

www.ingramcontent.com/pod-product-compliance
Lightning Source LLC
Chambersburg PA
CBHW022120170526
45157CB00004B/1703